Alexandra Adlawan

Wild Imagination

THE ADVENTURES OF MADDIE AND ALBERT

WRITTEN AND ILLUSTRATED BY ALEXANDRA ADLAWAN

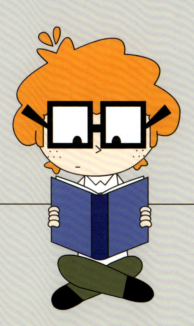

Hi, my name's Albert.

One of my favorite things to do is read.

It doesn't matter if it's for school or just for fun...

...reading is a great way to pass the time...

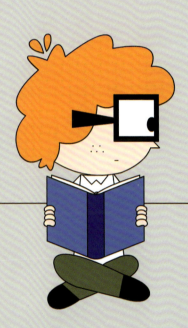

...there's just one problem about reading...

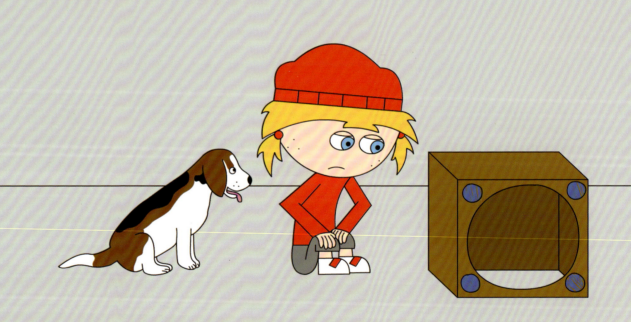

Author's Note

Alexandra Adlawan
is one of many amazing artists across the Autism spectrum.

Ever since her family can remember Alexandra has always had a wild imagination. She began to draw at a young age and created many characters and stories that she would share with her mom and dad. These drawings and storybooks can be found stored neatly in her work area. With Alexandra's publication of *"Wild Imagination, The Adventures of Maddie and Albert,"* her characters can finally see the light.

Pictured here with Alexandra is Dude (he's the one on the left). Dude is a *Good Dog Autism Companion*. Through his irrestible personality, Dude helps Alexandra navigate the world.

Alexandra would like to thank all of you for supporting her wild imagination. Until the next adventure...

Acknowledgements/Dedication

No two people have ever worked so hard to provide a nurturing environment for their child than my mom and dad. I want to thank them for helping me through the daily challenges of being a child on the Autism Spectrum. This book is as much a victory for them as it is for me. It is with their love and support that I am able to share with you my wild imagination.

My sister, Danielle, her husband John, my nephew Joe, and niece Julianne, were my elaborate characters' first audience. Thanks for being there for me.

Thank you to Jill, Ernie, Benjamin, Laura, Hayz, and Kat from Exceptional Minds - Vocational Center and Animation Studio for Young Adults on the Autism Spectrum. Your encouragement has made a huge difference.

And finally, special thanks to my teacher & mentor, Tawd b. Dorenfeld, whose patience and calming talent has helped me reach my dream of publishing this book.

Across the Spectrum

Text copyright © 2018 by Alexandra Adlawan
Illustrations copyright © 2018 by Alexandra Adlawan
All rights reserved.

FIRST EDITION 2018

No part of this book may be reproduced, scanned or distributed in any printed or electronic form without permission in writing from the publisher. Amazing Artists LLC, Long Beach, CA USA. Please do not participate in or encourage piracy of copyrighted materials in violation of the author's rights. Purchase only authorized editions.

ISBN 978-1-7324462-0-5

Library of Congress
Control Number: 2018947649

Printed and Bounded in China

Published by:
Amazing Artists LLC
2336 Heather Avenue, Long Beach, CA USA
www.amazingartists.online